W9-AMS-905

3 1192 00000

x551.2 Bende.L

Bender, Lionel.

Mountain   INTERIM SITE

N

x551.2 Bende.L

Bender, Lionel.

Mountain

THE STORY OF THE EARTH
MOUNTAIN

LIONEL BENDER

FRANKLIN WATTS

London · New York · Toronto · Sydney

EVANSTON PUBLIC LIBRARY
CHILDREN'S DEPARTMENT
1703 ORRINGTON AVENUE
EVANSTON, ILLINOIS 60201

© 1988 Franklin Watts

First published in Great Britain by
Franklin Watts
12a Golden Square
London W1

First published in the USA by
Franklin Watts Inc.
387 Park Avenue South
New York. N.Y. 10016

First published in Australia by
Franklin Watts Australia
14 Mars Road
Lane Cove
NSW 2066

UK ISBN 086313 737 7
US ISBN 0-531-10646-2
Library of Congress Catalog Card
No: 88-50370

Printed in Belgium

Consultant Dougal Dixon

Researched by Keith Lye

Designed by Ben White

Picture research Jan Croot

Illustrations
Peter Bull Art

Photographs
GeoScience Features 7, 21, 25, 29, 30
Alan Hutchinson Library 16, 23,
Keith Lye 11, 15
Science Photo Library 12
Survival Anglia 13, 18, 20
Swiss National Tourist Office 1
Dr. A.C. Waltham 17, 22
ZEFA *cover*, 10, 28

THE STORY OF THE EARTH
MOUNTAIN

LIONEL BENDER

CONTENTS

This book tells the story of a mountain. It shows how great forces inside the Earth create mountains. It also explains how the weather wears down or erodes mountains until they are flat. Our mountain starts beneath the ocean bed as hot liquid rock. Gradually it becomes part of a huge mass of land called a continent.

▽ Forces within the Earth push rocks on the ocean bed downward. Deep down, they start to melt. The hot rocks rise to form islands. Over millions of years the islands are pushed against a continent to form a group, or range, of mountains. The forces also crack rocks and crumple flat layers of rock into folds.

The story is divided into ten stages, as shown below. The first six stages tell how the mountain is created. Then we find out how the mountain is worn down. But that is not the end of the story. The worn rocks are gradually turned into new rocks. These will one day form new groups of mountains – a mountain range.

▽ A mountain does not last forever. Rain, wind, ice and rivers wear it down until it is nearly flat. As the worn material is carried downhill by rivers and bodies of ice, called glaciers, it breaks up into tiny pieces. Most of this material piles up on the ocean bed as pebbles, sand or mud. It is then pressed together to form hard rock.

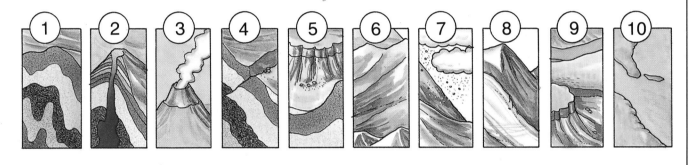

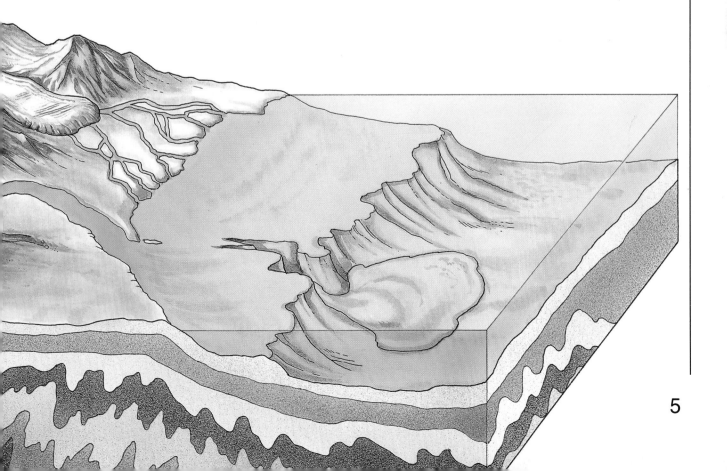

The mountain begins as layers of rocks beneath the ocean. The rocks are called sedimentary rocks, because they are made of sediments, that is bits of worn rock, including pebbles and mud.

Millions of years ago, currents in the water spread the sediments over the ocean bed. There they piled up in layers. The top layers pressed down on the sediments deep below until they became hard layers of rock. Now, forces beneath the ocean bed are starting to lift up the rock.

▷ Earth movements lift up layers of rock formed on ocean beds. The layers can be seen on bare valley walls. The Grand Canyon contains layer upon layer of rock known as sandstone. This is made up of sand and mud from a sea that once covered the area.

▽ 150 million years ago, these animals lived on the ocean bed. As they died, bits of their bones and shells were buried in the sediments. They were trapped as fossils in the rocks formed from the sediments.

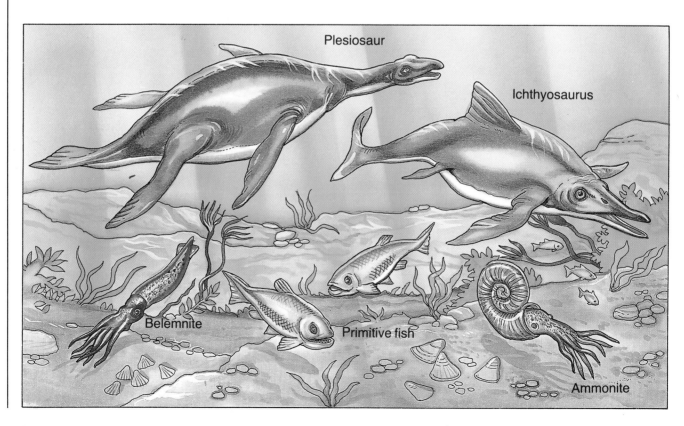

Plesiosaur

Ichthyosaurus

Belemnite

Primitive fish

Ammonite

The layers of rock on the ocean bed are slowly crushed together from the sides by Earth movements. This produces a line of weakness in the rocky "skin" or crust of the Earth. Along this line, great forces push huge slabs of the crust over one another. Some of the solid rock is melted by the heat deep within the Earth. The hot liquid rock pushes up through the weak spots to form a row of cone-shaped islands. Each island is a small volcano. One of these is our mountain.

▷The islands of Japan were formed from volcanoes that rose up from the ocean bed as a result of movements and forces in the Earth's crust. Japan still has several volcanoes, such as Mount Fuji, which erupt from time to time.

▽ The Earth's crust is hard and solid. It is made up of two types of plates of rock – those that lie beneath the seas and those that carry huge masses of land, the continents. Beneath the crust is the mantle, which is mainly hot liquid rock. The center of the Earth is called the core.

▽The outer layer of the Earth, the crust, is made up of slabs or plates that slowly move and grind against one another. When one plate slides over another, the plate underneath melts. The hot liquid rock pushes through the flat layers of rock on the ocean bed above.

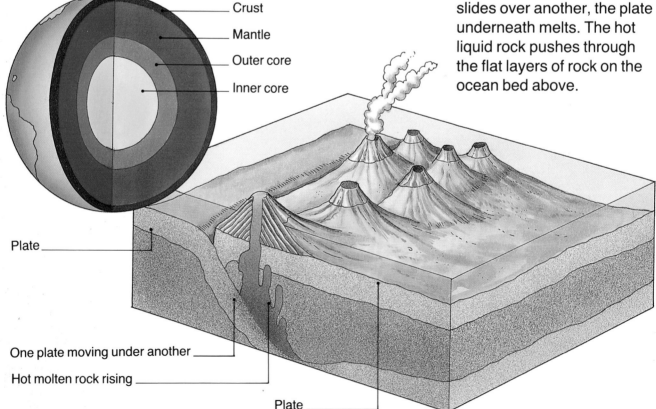

Crust

Mantle

Outer core

Inner core

Plate

One plate moving under another

Hot molten rock rising

Plate

As two of the slabs of the Earth's crust slide over one another, the chain of volcanic islands crashes into a giant continent. The islands and the rocks on the surrounding ocean bed become crushed and crumpled by the force. The layers of rock start to bulge upward, just as sheets of paper do if their opposite edges are pushed together. Slowly but surely, the mountain grows up along the edge of the continent.

◁These rock layers in the Andes Mountains of South America were once flat. They became folded as two plates collided.

▽Movements in the Earth's crust are happening now. For example, a plate is being pushed under the west coast of South America. Deep down, the plate sinking beneath South America is melting. Molten rock is rising through the Andes Mountains. Some of it reaches the surface through volcanoes, such as this one, El Misti, in southern Peru.

Folding and cracking

▷Giant slabs of rock sometimes move up or down along faults. When the blocks are pushed upward between faults, they form block mountains. The Grand Tetons are a range of block mountains. It is in Wyoming.

Occasionally, blocks of land slip down between faults. Steep-sided valleys called rift valleys are formed in this way.

◁A long crack runs for hundreds of miles across the land in California. It is called the San Andreas Fault. This fault is the border between two plates which are moving alongside each other. When they move, earthquakes occur. The fault runs across the land and under the lakes at the top of this picture.

The mountain now rests on a plate carrying a continent. It is surrounded by other mountains. Pressures and movements within and beneath the plate continue to make the mountain rise. Each year it grows an inch or more taller.

The rock layers also become more folded, and cracks start to appear in them. The cracks are called faults. They split the mountain range into blocks, and these grind against each other.

Besides being forced upward, the mountain range is also being twisted and bent. Along one border, the plate on which the range rests is sliding over another plate. Along the opposite border, it is grinding against a third plate. Two continents are moving toward one another.

New ocean beds and volcanic islands are being crumpled up in between the continents. Gradually, our mountain is changing shape and the range is being bent into a huge curve across the surface of the Earth.

▷ Around the Mediterranean Sea, plate movements have created volcanoes in southern Italy. One of them is the volcanic island of Stromboli. The movement of Africa has also squeezed up rocks into mountain ranges. Bits of land have been broken away from Europe to form such islands as Corsica and Sardinia.

◁ A huge plate carrying Africa has been grinding against Europe for millions of years. This movement is still going on. Millions of years from now, the Mediterranean Sea may close up. The rocks on the sea bed between Africa and Europe will then be squeezed up to form a new fold mountain range.

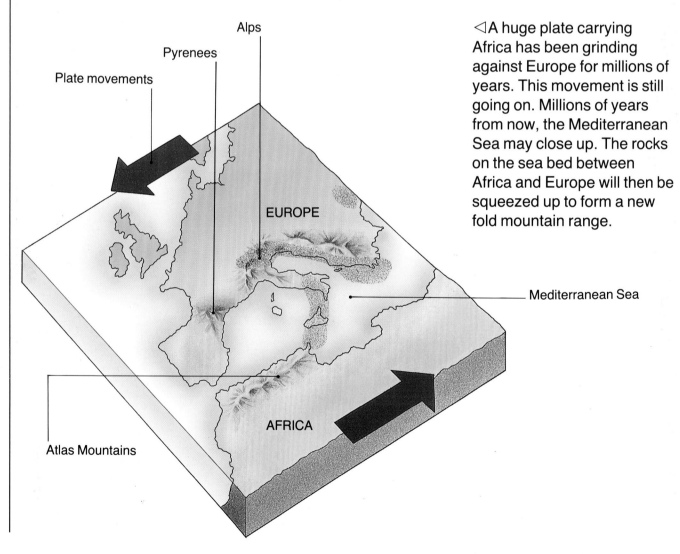

Plate movements · Pyrenees · Alps · EUROPE · Mediterranean Sea · Atlas Mountains · AFRICA

The mountain reaches its greatest size when the two continents crash into each other. The collision causes its layers of rock to become more folded and cracked than ever before.

The mountain ranges that have formed along the coast of each continent fuse together. They form a mass of land that is so solid and strong that all movement of the plates ceases. And so the mountain stops growing.

▷Annapurna is one of the highest peaks in the Himalayan range. The range was formed some 60 million years ago when the plate on which India rests collided with the southern Asian plate.

▽These mountains in Scotland reached their greatest size 370 million years ago when the continents of North America and Europe collided. The continents have since split apart and the mountains are no longer growing.

△This marmot lives in mountains in North America. During the summer it feeds on plants and builds up a store of fat. It sleeps through the winter, using up the fat for energy to stay alive.

Mountain wildlife

Life is hard for animals in high mountain areas, which are cold and windy. Many animals that live there have thick coats to keep them warm. Most large animals, such as bighorns (wild sheep) and wild goats, are good rock climbers. Many small animals, such as hares, hibernate (sleep) during the cold winter months. Others store food in summer and eat it in winter.

▽Large birds, such as American condors, can fly in the windy mountain air. Small birds usually stay close to the ground. Some hunting animals, such as pumas and wolves, go to high mountain areas in the summer. But in the winter, they go down to the valleys where they find shelter.

Even as the mountain is being formed, the forces of the weather start to wear it away. On the high slopes, where it is cold and wet, frost and ice attack the rocks. Water that trickles between the rocks freezes and turns to ice. The ice presses on the sides of the cracks and widens them. Finally, the rocks break apart and bits tumble down the slope. When the rock cracks, it sounds like a pistol being fired.

▽ Rocks in deserts, as here in Death Valley, California, are broken up by heating and cooling. Although deserts are usually dry places, storms may occur every few years. The land is flooded and the water washes away the broken rocks.

◁ Rocks broken up by frost action tumble downhill. They often collect in big piles at the bottom of steep slopes. Mosses and lichens, which are simple plants that do not produce flowers, grow on the damp rock surfaces. They help to break up the rocks.

21

Wind, rain and rivers carry away the loose rocks. As streams rush down the steep slopes, they roll the rocks along their beds. The streams not only push the rocks downhill, but they also wear out deep grooves or valleys. This is because the moving stones wear away the land.

Large bodies of ice called glaciers also carry rocks as they slide downhill. Rocks frozen in the ice scrape at the land. In this way, glaciers, too, wear away the mountain.

▷Glaciers form on mountains from snow that is pressed into ice. The dark lines on this glacier are loose rocks that have tumbled down from the rocky slopes.

◁In the summer, mountain streams often contain only a trickle of water. But in the spring, when the snow and ice on the mountaintops start to melt, the streams become torrents of rushing water. The rocks swept along by water loosen and carry away rocks on the beds of the streams. The moving rocks are ground down into smaller and smaller pieces.

Over millions of years, the tall mountain is steadily worn down. Most of the rocks that formed the mountain are ground down into pebbles, sand and mud. These sediments are carried away by running water, glaciers and the wind into the ocean. There they pile up in layers on the ocean bed. The worn down mountain consists of hills, shallow valleys and some stumps of hard rock. A few jagged stumps are the remains of the old volcanoes.

▽When hot liquid rock pushes up under a mountain range, it hardens into a rock called granite. When the layers of softer rock above it are worn away, the granite is seen on the surface. Granite is a tough rock. But it, too, finally wears away.

▷Granite stumps are sometimes left behind when a mountain range is worn away. Granite often contains cracks. Rainwater makes these cracks bigger. Finally, the rock crumbles. The picture shows a granite tor, or outcrop, in southwest England.

Soft rock

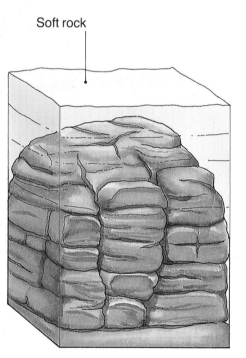

Granite tor

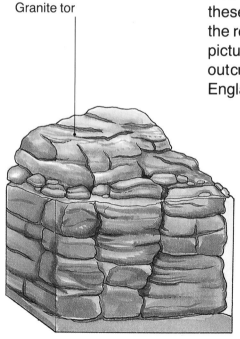

The mountain range is eventually worn down so much that it becomes a completely flat area of land. The rock here is so solid that it will never again be forced up into mountains or disturbed by Earth movements. The area is known as a shield.

The sediments that have been worn away and carried out to sea, however, will one day form new mountains. The cycle of building and wearing away of mountains never stops.

◁The Icelandic Shield covers much of Iceland. Many very old and very hard rocks are found there. Some of these rocks contain valuable metals, such as iron, copper, gold and silver.

▽A shield is a low-lying region containing flat areas, low hills and many lakes. Bare rock with little or no soil covers large parts of the shield. Rivers flow slowly over the land. Along the rivers, much of the land is swampy. The rivers sometimes overflow and cause floods.

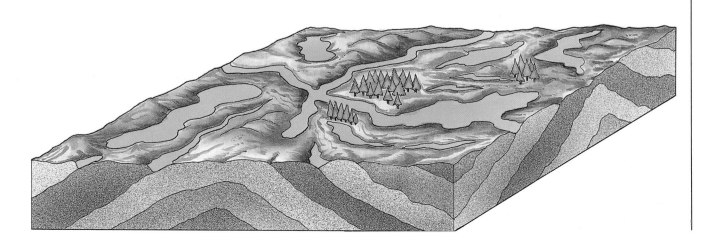

Mountains and people

People used to think of mountains as dangerous places. Travel was difficult and few people lived there. But today many mountain areas have good roads and tunnels for cars and trains. Many people now spend their vacations in the mountains. Some go there for winter sports, such as skiing. Others enjoy walking and climbing. Farmers graze their animals on mountain slopes in summer. But they lead the animals down to the shelter of the valleys when winter starts.

▽ Building villages and farms on mountain slopes is difficult. Here in Nepal, people have made flat areas of land, called terraces, on the slopes. These terraces look like steps. Without them, the rain would wash away all the soil, making the land unsafe for houses and useless for growing crops.

△ Roads across mountains are built with
many bends and in places with tunnels. A
road that went straight up the mountainside
would be too steep for vehicles to drive up.
Falls of rocks and snow often block the roads.

Glossary

Block mountain A mountain formed when a block of land is lifted up between long lines of faults in the Earth's crust.

Canyon A deep, steep-sided valley.

Continent A large land mass. The world has seven continents – North and South America, Europe, Asia, Africa, Australia and Antarctica.

Core The central part of the Earth, The core measures about 6,920 km (4,300 miles) across.

Crust The Earth's outer shell. The crust that supports continents is 35–40 km (22–25 miles) thick. The crust beneath the oceans is about 6 km (4 miles) thick.

Earthquake A sudden movement in the Earth's crust. They are common in areas where mountains are being formed.

Fault A break in the rocks of the Earth's crust along which the rocks have moved.

Folds Loops in rock layers caused by sideways pressure within the crust.

Fossil Evidence of ancient life in rocks, such as impressions of shells and bones, logs which have been turned into stone, and dinosaur footprints.

Glacier A river of ice that forms high up on mountains and flows downhill under its own weight.

Granite A rock formed when molten material hardens underground.

Landslide Downhill movements of loose rocks and soil.

Mantle The part of the Earth between the crust and the core. It is about 2,900 km (1,802 miles) thick.

Plate Part of the solid outside layer of the Earth, including the crust and the top part of the mantle. The plates float on a molten layer of rock in the mantle.

Rock The substances which make up the Earth. Some form from molten material. Others form from sediments on ocean beds.

Valley A groove or channel in the land caused by Earth movements or carved by rivers or glaciers.

Volcanoes Holes in the ground from which molten rock spews out; also the mountains formed from the molten rock.

Facts about mountains

The world's highest range is the Himalaya-Karakoram in Asia. It contains 96 of the world's highest peaks. This range is called the "Roof of the World".

Mount Everest is the world's tallest mountain measured from sea level. It is 8,848 m (29,029 ft) high. It is in the Himalayan range. The Himalayan range also includes Kanchenjunga, the world's third highest mountain, at 8,598 m (22,208 ft).

Mount Godwin Austin which is also called K2, is the world's second highest peak. It is in the Karakoram range, which is joined to the Himalayan range. It is 8,611 m (28,250 ft) high.

The world's highest mountain, measured from its base on the ocean bed to its peak, is Mauna Loa, a volcano in Hawaii. It has a total height of 10,203 m (33,476 ft). But 5,998 m (19,678 ft) is hidden underwater.

Cerro Aconcagua in the Andes Mountains in Argentina is the highest volcanic mountain measured from sea level. It is an extinct (dead) volcano. At 6,960 m (22,835 ft) high, it is the highest mountain in the Americas.

Indonesia has 167 volcanic mountains, 77 of which have erupted in historic times. This is more than any other country.

The Andes Mountains form the world's longest mountain range. It runs the entire length of western South America, some 5,120 km (3,200 miles).

▷ Mount Everest, the world's highest mountain, stands on the border between Nepal and China. It was first climbed on May 29, 1953. The climbers were Sir Edmund Hillary, a New Zealander, and Tenzing Norgay, a Sherpa guide who was born in Nepal. It has been climbed many times since 1953.

Index

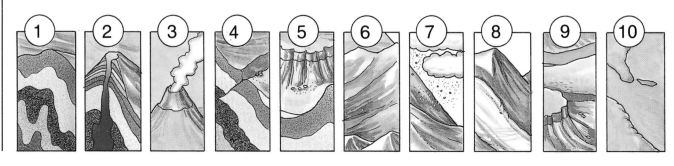